D0589139

POCKET STUDY SKILLS

*Series Editor: **Kate Williams**, Oxford Brookes University, UK*
Illustrations by Sallie Godwin

For the time-pushed student, the *Pocket Study Skills* pack a lot of advice into a little book. Each guide focuses on a single crucial aspect of study giving you step-by-step guidance, handy tips and clear advice on how to approach the important areas which will continually be at the core of your studies.

Published

14 Days to Exam Success
Blogs, Wikis, Podcasts and More
Brilliant Writing Tips for Students
Getting Critical
Planning Your Essay
Planning Your PhD
Reading and Making Notes
Referencing and Understanding Plagiarism
Science Study Skills
Success in Groupwork

Further titles are planned

Pocket Study Skills
Series Standing Order
ISBN 978-0230-21605-1
(outside North America only)

You can receive future titles in this series as they are published by placing a standing order. Please contact your bookseller or, in case of difficulty, write to us at the address below with your name and address, the title of the series and the ISBN quoted above.

Customer Services Department, Macmillan Distribution Ltd Houndmills, Basingstoke, Hampshire RG21 6XS England

14 DAYS TO EXAM SUCCESS

POCKET STUDY SKILLS

Lucinda Becker

palgrave
macmillan

First published 2010 by
PALGRAVE MACMILLAN

Palgrave Macmillan in the UK is an imprint of Macmillan Publishers Limited, registered in England, company number 785998, of Houndmills, Basingstoke, Hampshire RG21 6XS.

Palgrave Macmillan in the US is a division of St Martin's Press LLC, 175 Fifth Avenue, New York, NY 10010.

Palgrave Macmillan is the global academic imprint of the above companies and has companies and representatives throughout the world.

Palgrave® and Macmillan® are registered trademarks in the United States, the United Kingdom, Europe and other countries

ISBN-13: 978-0-230-24910-3

This book is printed on paper suitable for recycling and made from fully managed and sustained forest sources. Logging, pulping and manufacturing processes are expected to conform to the environmental regulations of the country of origin.

A catalogue record for this book is available from the British Library.

A catalog record for this book is available from the Library of Congress.

Printed in China

Contents

Acknowledgements

I am grateful to Sallie Godwin for her imaginative illustrations. Many thanks also to Flissy, Annie, Matthew and Tom for their advice, ideas and enthusiasm.

How to use this book

Success in exams is not just about what you know: it is about how you use what you know. This book is designed to help you remember as much as you can, but also to use that knowledge in the most effective way.

Unplanned revision can be deathly dull, and that is not conducive to remembering what you need to recall in an exam. By following the plan for each day, you will keep your brain active and geared up to perform in the final exams. By varying your tasks you will be in the best position possible as you move towards the exams.

You can make a huge difference to your performance in the 14 days before an exam. If you have longer than 2 weeks, you can take more time to complete each day's task, but a fortnight will be enough time to marshal the facts and ideas that will improve your performance radically.

Take it steady: for each day there is a checklist of things to do, an extended section which covers a key aspect of exam preparation, and a page or so which will offer you some extra help and support as you move forward. You will not need to produce a revision timetable – this book does that for you – but you will need to set aside time each day to work through the tasks set out here.

Taking stock

For the first 5 days of your revision you will be sorting and storing information – this will give you the material you need to make the impression you want in the exam. After that, you will be using your stored information to work on essay plans and to work through past papers until Day 10, when you will focus more tightly on the exam, giving yourself some mock exams. Day 11 is an easier day, and then you will take a run up to the exams with a structured series of tasks.

The key to success is to keep going in those first few days – think of it like a construction project. You are taking down the wall of information, brick by brick, discarding some bricks you do not need, and reassembling the bricks into a new shape for the exam.

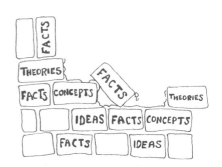

Day 1

Things to do today

☐ Look through example papers for your course so that you know where you are going. You might have been given some examples, or you might find them in the library or on the website for your university or college.

☐ Make sure that you are clear about the division of marks between coursework and exams. This may vary from course to course. Although you will want to shine in every exam, you might feel less pressurised if you discover that the exam for a particular course only counts for 30% of the mark; if it counts for 100% of the mark for one course, your focus will be far greater on that portion of revision.

☐ Check and double check the exam timetable and put copies of it in your diary, on your fridge door – anywhere and everywhere you can.

☐ Divide your material into eight sections, based on a natural division of your courses; if you are doing just a few courses, you will be able to divide the material for each course into several sections. Don't worry that some sections of material will seem 'easier' than others: that will give you some easier days as you progress, which is a good thing. Eight sections will give you the division of material you need to work through the revision process in 14 days; if you have more or less time than that, you can make more or fewer sections of material.

Types of exam

The type of exam you are facing will affect the way you revise, so here is some guidance.

1 Multiple choice exams

In a multiple choice exam you will face, for each question, a set of answers, of which you must usually choose just one. For revision, this means learning as many facts and ideas as possible. For any set of possible answers, there will usually be one which is fairly obviously false, several which are plausible but not right, and one or two which look correct. The secret is to examine these last two possibilities closely so that you choose the right one. In the exam, you don't need to answer the questions in order. Instead, you could work through the paper, choosing the answers to the questions you find easiest, then spend longer on the more difficult questions. Try not to rush the first stage: it is too easy to tick the wrong box in your haste. Leave yourself more time than you might usually do to check your answers: the speed of these exams can easily catch you out.

2 Short answer exams

These are perhaps the easiest exams. You will need fewer facts at your fingertips than in a multiple choice exam, but you will have to know how to plan precisely and write succinctly. Your plan for each answer might not be as elaborate as for a full essay exam – perhaps just a set of bullet points – but it will be essential if you are not to get carried away and find that you have spent too long on one answer and included too much material. Some students prefer to write their answers using bullet points, too, so that they remain clear and precise in their writing.

3 Essay exams

These are perhaps the most traditional exams, asking for one or more essays in two or three hours. The good news is that they require, funnily enough, the least amount of knowledge. Instead, they ask you to use your knowledge in answering questions. Planning and practice will be crucial, and learning what you are really being asked is also essential – more about this on Day 5.

4 Blended exams

Some exams ask for a combination of multiple choice, short answers and one or two essays. They require all the skills you will be developing by using this guide, but you will need to be ready to take charge. You might choose to work on the most tiring section first (usually the longer essay) and then move back to the multiple choice section, to get your brain back up to speed before tackling the short answer section. As you practise, giving yourself some mock exams, you will find the best way for you – and you need to stick to this in the exam.

The first step

Well done! This has been a hard-work day, and you have taken the first, important step: you are now organised and ready to move on, safe in the knowledge that you can achieve the best possible result in the time available. These basics are vital, so don't skimp on them: if you have not completed it all today, set aside a little time tomorrow to catch up with yourself.

Exams are not designed as traps to fail you. Your tutors are willing you to succeed, and will have designed the exam to give you the most help possible. They are simply trying to take a snapshot of where you are now; exams give you the best chance to shine, to show that you are developing in a subject area and are keen to succeed. Such ambition is always rewarded.

What nobody tells you as they teach you is that no student could know, or would ever be expected to know, 100% of the material on a course. In most cases, you will already know at least 50% of what you need to remember as you begin to revise, and you only need to aim to know about 70–80% of the material for most courses. The credit will come from how you use your knowledge, and that is what you will be doing from now on.

Things to do today

☐ Take Section 1 of the material you divided yesterday. Reduce the material by working through it, at a reasonably fast pace, and making revision notes, the briefer the better, ready to make some revision cards.

☐ Look up anything you are unclear about, but only look up the minimum amount of information, at points where you now realise, looking back on the material, that you have not understood something. Only do this if you believe that it is essential for you to know this piece of material. This is revision, not new learning, and so in some places you will be able to make a judgement that a certain section of material can be left behind, as you can safely assume that you will not need to use it in the exams.

☐ Take a break. This is an easier day than some – you are only tackling one section of your material – but that is deliberate. You need time to find your best rhythm of working, and to mull over quietly what you have been working on today.

Testing yourself in the early stages

Later on, you will be able to test your knowledge by planning some practice exam answers. At this stage, you simply need to consider how much you actually know. This comes in part from making notes: be firm with yourself and only write in your revision notes the essentials; as you go through the material, keep on your shoulder a 'know-it gremlin'. That is, if you feel familiar with the facts as you write them out in brief, make a conscious point of noting this to yourself. By the time you have reduced the material to revision notes, you will have a good sense of how much you know already. Keep your know-it gremlin on your shoulder throughout – it will guide you when it comes to later revision.

Give yourself a break once you have produced the revision notes for a section, then go back and be brutal: highlight the sections you really need, and cross out all of the notes that you know so well you will never need to consider them again, and any notes which you can see now are superfluous to your needs.

Once you have your revision notes in place, you will be ready to reduce them even further by producing revision cards. Making revision cards is an art, and it is one you will need to practise as you move forward. You are aiming to produce small (6" x 4") postcard-sized cards, with only essential information on them. This might be a list of facts, or some quotes to remember, or an essay plan, or a series of connections which you want to make in the exam.

As the exam approaches, in the last day or so, you will also make 'last minute' revision cards. There will probably be only one of these for each exam, and they will only include those few facts which you believe you will never be able to remember for longer than a few minutes. As soon as you get into the exam you will jot down these facts on your planning pages, so that you can relax and focus on the task ahead of you.

Before you look at the next few pages, think about everything you have ever heard (or learned) about Shakespeare's play *Romeo and Juliet*. Then read on to see how revision cards work ...

What is 'essential information'?

It is easy to suggest that you only note down the essential information from your course notes; it can be hard to do in practice. You will need to take a light touch with your full notes as you reduce them, and one way to do this is to imagine all of the material as a beach. As you wander across the beach, every now and then you will see a rock sticking up out the sand – a piece of information or an idea that really sticks out for you. It might be that you remember it vividly from your lessons, or that it is something that helps make sense of an idea for you. In your notes, these rocks are often the short sentences that you noted down to sum up a whole section of a lecture, or the first sentence you wrote as you listened in a classroom.

As you progress you will find it easier to see the rocks standing up from the sand. The trick is to scan your notes, skim reading sections and all the time asking yourself, 'What is the sand that I am leaving behind? Where are the rocks in these notes?'

Revision cards: how they might look

Imagine that you are revising for an exam about Shakespeare's play *Romeo and Juliet*. Here are examples of cards you might need to make – note that every card has a title so that you can glance at it in the future and test yourself.

Revision card: an example of a basic card

> ### Romeo and Juliet: facts
>
> - *Romeo and Juliet* written (probably) in 1594 or 1595.
> - Already a well-known story – from Arthur Brooke's poem (1562).
> - It has a prologue, like Greek chorus – in sonnet form.
> - Montague and Capulet – the two families – reconciled in the end.
> - Imaginative language and comic relief used.
> - Luhrmann's film (1996) – modern take on the play.

Revision card: an example of a connections card

You would need to know Shakespeare's plays to make these particular connections, but connections like these will be clear to you from your own course.

> ### Romeo and Juliet: connections
>
> - Typical tragedy – reconciliation at the end – like *King Lear*.
> - Young lovers being wayward – like *A Midsummer Night's Dream*.
> - Jealous love leading to death – like *Othello*.
> - Young woman dying – like *Othello* and *King Lear*.
> - Idea of fate controlling events – like *Macbeth*.
> - Young man struggling with his destiny – like *Hamlet*, perhaps?

Revision card: an example of an essay plan card

> Essay topic: Is *Romeo and Juliet* suitable
> for study at GCSE level?
>
> *Yes, because:*
> → the main characters are young
> → it is romantic, and tragic
> → modern film adaptations make it accessible
> → it covers issues which are still relevant today.
>
> *No, because:*
> → maybe the lovers are too young to be acceptable?
> → religion and fate are invoked – too complicated?
> → the language is challenging, would this be a barrier?

Revision card: an example of a last-minute card

This card is not attempting to capture a whole course; it is a way to remember, just before you go into an exam, the random facts which you know you keep forgetting.

> ▸ Arthur Brooke – 1562
> ▸ Written 1594/5
> ▸ Romeo's best friend – Mercutio
> ▸ Modern film – *Romeo + Juliet* – Baz Luhrmann, 1996

Getting to know your 'know-it gremlin'

Gremlins are usually thought of as mythical little creatures that mischievously make things go wrong. Your know-it gremlin is quite different, and can be your greatest ally in revising. It will help you to be confident. Imagine this little creature sitting on your shoulder, whispering in your ear 'You know it!'

Your gremlin will do this when you test yourself on a detailed revision card and are ready to reduce it to a much briefer card. He will do it again to give you the confidence to set aside a card once you know it, and when you come to planning essays he will be there, whispering in your ear as you produce the best possible plan.

You will know when you are ignoring your gremlin: you will be rereading a card over and over again, with no real sense of how much you know; or panicking and going back to material that you mastered days ago.

We all have a know-it gremlin. Yours is whispering to you when you suddenly find yourself relaxing, relieved that you have lodged something soundly in your brain. If you can learn to recognise how this feels, you are firmly on the road to success.

Things to do today

☐ Reduce your revision notes for Section 1 of your material to revision cards. Be bold: only include the essentials on each revision card, with your 'know-it gremlin' firmly on your shoulder.

☐ Reduce Section 2 of your material to revision notes.

You are now into the swing of revision: sifting through the material you have, pulling out the important information and making revision notes, leaving them overnight and then reducing them onto revision cards. You will carry this process on right up until Day 11, and it will be the core of your revision. Almost without realising it is happening, you will be learning as you go and remembering as you write, so that you can emerge at the end with the information you need to succeed at your command.

The rhythm of your revision

It is simply not possible to work at 100% efficiency for hours and hours on end. All of us need to take a rest at times, and you will need to learn how you work best.

The easiest way to discover your best working rhythm is to time yourself: check how many pages of material you reduce into revision notes in the first 20 minutes of your revision session today, and then the second 20 minutes, and so on. You will find that at some point your work rate drops dramatically. This will vary from person to person, but when you have pinpointed the 'drop point' for you, you will know when to take a break. As you revise more, you may well be able to work efficiently for longer, so check yourself in this way every couple of days.

'Taking a break' might be just that: a cup of tea, a walk about, maybe some chocolate and a complete rest from work for some time. If this is what you need, then take this type of break. A word of warning, though: try to avoid doing things in the break that will lead you too far away from revision. Checking a few emails, with a time limit, might be useful; logging on to Facebook and finding that an hour has gone by is far less useful! You need to be ready to return to your revision as soon as your brain has cleared and you feel less tired.

Of course, taking a break might not mean having to leave revision behind. It can be equally beneficial (and more productive) to simply change your task. If you are working on revision cards, then go back to making revision notes for the next section, or, in the later stages, produce a few essay plans.

Be true to yourself

Some people are naturally very methodical, planning each challenge in detail and working through the tasks in a regular way. By the time they reach an exam, they have spent weeks, maybe months, familiarising themselves with the material. Others take a last-minute approach, cramming for exams in the last few days, or hours, and relying on flair and adrenaline to get them through.

Both of these approaches can work: methodical workers have the reassurance that they are progressing smoothly, but can get bored with the material and struggle to retain all of the information; last-minute workers have to hope they are not struck down with 'flu, and are more likely to miss vital information.

You can improve your performance. If you are methodical, varying your tasks regularly will reduce the dangers of boredom; if you are a last-minute worker, the rigid structure of this guide will keep you motivated. However, whichever type of student you are, there is very little point in trying to be other than you are. The way of working that has seen you through life so far will carry on working for you, because it is what suits you.

Taking stock

You have now achieved the most important part of your revision: you have got to grips with the process, and are well on your way to achieving the ultimate goal: succeeding in the exam.

I know how my exams will look ☑

I know where they all are ☑

I have divided all of my material ☑

I can pace myself ☑

I can reduce my notes ☑

I have made my revision cards ☑

I can see how course work and exams work ☑

I recognise my 'know it' gremlin ☑

Things to do today

☐ Reduce your revision notes for Section 2 of your material to revision cards.

☐ Reduce Section 3 of your material to revision notes.

By now you will be getting into the rhythm of your revising. Each day will include repetitious tasks, but what makes it interesting is that the material is different from day to day. Some days will be quite easy, if you already feel comfortable with the material; other days will be more challenging. By overlapping material, as you begin to work it up into essay plans and, later, into further reduced cards, you will be refreshing your memory and working the material as you press on ahead.

On the days when you feel less familiar with the material you might need to refer to some secondary material to make things clear to you, and this can bring benefits and dangers …

Secondary sources: books and journals

These should be used very sparingly during your revision. You have your notes and handouts from your course: going to other sources, such as books, journals and the internet, can be a huge and distracting time waster.

If you realise that you absolutely need to check out an area (if, for example, your notes are unclear or you know you did not really understand the topic in the first place), try following these guidelines for texts:

▶ Know before you go to the library or resource centre exactly *what* you need to look at and *why* you are looking at it. You must identify beforehand the gaps in your knowledge that you are trying to fill.

▶ Make a list of books to look at and stick to it – no wandering the aisles in search of inspiration!

▶ Use the index and table of contents of each book to give you a sense of how much it might help you and as quick guides to its contents.

▶ Photocopy only the pages you really need and then use them as if they were your condensed notes (reducing them to revision cards), but skim read them first before you make the commitment to photocopy them: do you really need them?

Secondary sources: the internet

The internet is the single most alluring time waster known to students, so be very careful as you use it during revision. Try following these guidelines for the internet:

 ▶ Avoid Google: it will bring up too many site options.
 ▶ Instead, ask your tutors to recommend specific sections of particular sites.
 ▶ Make a 'shopping list' in advance so you know where you are going to look.
 ▶ Print off the pages you think you need, and use them just as you would your lecture notes.
 ▶ Don't file the pages until you have pulled them apart and reduced them to brief revision cards; they can otherwise lurk and distract you.
 ▶ Set yourself a strict time limit for an internet session and stick to it.
 ▶ Keep your know-it gremlin on your shoulder at all times – there is no point in printing off material you already know.

Just how much do you need to know?

The quick answer is: probably not nearly as much as you think you need to know. If exams are all about how you use your knowledge, then the most important task in your revision will not be cramming more and more material into your head, but using the material and grasping concepts.

Each day, take the time to move away from your revision cards. Take a topic where you have mastered most of what is on the revision cards and brainstorm the topic. You are not tying yourself to lots of facts, but instead looking at the bigger picture: this is what most exams are designed to test.

From Day 6, I will be encouraging you to produce essay and exam plans. These will stop you from getting bored because they use your knowledge, and they will give you a much clearer idea of what you know, and – more importantly – what you actually need to know.

Here is an example of a brainstorm on a topic. There are not many facts, but there are ideas that are essential to grasping the bigger picture:

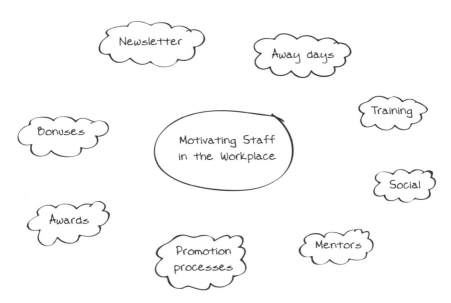

Things to do today

☐ Reduce your revision notes for Section 3 of your material to revision cards.

☐ Reduce Section 4 of your material to revision notes.

From now on you are going to be working on further reductions. Your revision cards will not stay as they are: you will need to be more active in how you use them. There is no set pattern for this, but each day take the time to test yourself on a batch of your cards (you do not need to divide them into each section's cards for this; just test yourself on as many as you can for the time you have available). Be confident about what you know: when you have a few spare minutes, pick up some of the cards, check the title of the card, cover it up and try to recite as much as you can remember. Once you have done this three or four times and feel that you know most of what is on some of the cards, you can reduce them still further, and use fewer cards for each section of material.

Here are three revision cards on the subject of the 2008/9 financial recession, followed by an example of how they might be reduced once you have tested yourself on them three or four times:

> - Previous recession was a manufacturing recession, in the late 1980s. The current recession is a credit/banking recession.
> - Triggered by 'sub-prime' mortgages in the USA, but deeper problems than that.
> - Lack of confidence in the financial sector – contraction of the money markets.
> - Inter-bank loans dried up.

> - Started in USA but rapidly spread – seen as a threat to emerging markets in the East.
> - Britain hit because we were intertwined with USA banks and often underwrote their loans (high street banking still profitable, though).
> - Our govt. accused of not regulating the banking industry tightly enough.
> - Small businesses especially affected.

- Financial 'solutions' in Britain include reduction in VAT, bail-out of big banks, and 'quantitative easing' of the economy.
- Barclays and HSBC did not receive government bail-out, but remain profitable.
- Most agree that VAT reduction made little difference.
- Britain slow to come out of recession compared to other countries – political problem for the government.
- Bankers' big bonuses cause uproar.

Here is an example of a reduced revision card for these three, after successful testing:

- Manufacturing recession → credit crunch recession.
- USA → rest of the world (Britain coming out slower than others).
- Problem of financial sector regulations (and still big banker bonuses).
- VAT, bank bail-outs and quantitative easing → but criticism of government measure.
- Small businesses still have problems.

From now on, you would put the first three cards away and only revise from this final card. These headings should prompt you to the full set of information in that area. If you find that they don't, check back to your other cards for a moment to check the details. You will do this less and less as time goes on. When you are confident about knowing the reduced card, put it firmly to one side. As the pile of cards gets smaller, you will know that you are making progress!

Essay exams: what the questions mean …

The first thing to work out is what an essay title is actually asking you to do: the words used in the title are crucial. Only after that do you think about planning, which we will cover tomorrow. Here are some of the most **common keywords** used in essay titles:

Keyword	What you are expected to do
Compare	Highlight similarities (and perhaps differences) and, sometimes, offer a preference for one option or another.
Contrast	Bring out the differences between two topics, or two aspects of a topic.
Discuss/Consider	This is the widest possible instruction: you will be considering several aspects of the topic, and perhaps developing an argument.
Examine	This is generally a little easier. You are being asked to look in detail at the topic, but will not necessarily be expected to develop an argument.
Explore	This is similar to 'examine', except that you will range more widely, but still in great detail.
Describe	This is very specific, and you must follow the detail in the title carefully to make sure that you only describe what is relevant.

Keyword	What you are expected to do
State	This is usually used for briefer essays, where you will be describing something (usually a series of facts) but in a less extended way than if you were asked to 'describe'.
Analyse	This requires you to divide a subject up and look at each part of the topic in an analytical way. This is often used to evaluate several options given in the title.
Explain	This is similar to 'analyse', but usually with a sense that you are looking at one process or area of a topic, rather than dividing it up into many aspects.
Trace	This is often used for factual essays, where you are describing something, aiming to explain how something has developed.
Outline	This is similar to 'trace', except that you are usually covering a broader topic. You are being asked to make general points about an area.
Summarise	Here you are being asked to bring a subject under control, to show your understanding of the topic by being able to put forward its key points briefly.
Evaluate	This one is tricky: rather than being tempted to describe the topic, you are expected to use your knowledge to make a judgement about a topic or an opinion.

Six ways to feel good

Everyone needs encouragement when they are revising. Here are six ways to make yourself feel better if your enthusiasm starts to dip:

1 Brainstorm an area you haven't revised yet. It will remind you of how much you already know and boost your confidence.

2 Take half an hour to remind yourself that there is a world beyond your revision – Facebook is a great way to do this.

3 Make a firm date to do something relaxing and/or exciting a few days after your exams finish.

4 Make a 'happy pot'. Write notes to yourself, or jot down inspirational quotes, fold them and keep them in a pot, so that you can dip in and be inspired whenever you need it.

5 If you live with friends, make a shared happy pot for you all, with encouraging notes to each other.

6 Keep in touch by email with a friend who is not studying your subject (so that you won't bog each other down in the detail) – you can email from time to time if you need an encouraging word.

Things to do today

☐ Reduce your revision notes for Section 4 of your material to revision cards.

☐ Reduce Section 5 of your material to revision notes.

☐ Reduce your pile of revision cards (as many as you have time to do). You will do some of these each day, so that you gradually see the pile reducing.

☐ Begin working on essay plans.

There are two ways to reduce your pile of revision cards: you could follow the guide on Day 5, so that you end up with far fewer cards, or, if you feel more confident in an area, you could go straight to making a detailed essay plan for it. At this stage, you could just make up a general essay title for a subject. If you find that you have left very little out, all of the topic cards can be discarded and you can revise from your essay plan.

Essay planning

It is far easier to remember things if you are using your knowledge, and essay plans are a good way to do this. Even if most of your exams are multiple choice, or short answer exams, planning can help you to use and so more easily recall the material you need. You will come to know the best method for you as you practise. Below are examples of how different methods might be used to answer the essay question: 'Consider the use of alternative energy sources in the UK to combat global warming'.

Creating a brainstorm

A brainstorm is not a complete planning method in itself; it is a way to help your brain to produce a series of good ideas.

- In the centre of the page, put the central idea (this would usually consist of a few key words from the essay title or area of discussion).
- Around the page, and in no particular order, jot down other thoughts that arise from that one central idea. You can be as wide-ranging as you like, and not every idea has to be perfect: often irrelevant ideas might be abandoned later, but will have helped you initially by pushing your mind towards other areas of thought.
- Once you feel that you have drained your brain of all the ideas you might want to cover, be firm and cross out any ideas/thoughts/facts which, on reflection, are not going to help you in your essay.

Brainstorm example

Using a brainstorm

You are now left with good, solid ideas on which to base a fuller plan. They will not be in any order, or developed to any great extent, so you may like to use one of the other methods described here to make a fuller, more detailed plan from which to write.

Some students always use a brainstorm as the first stage in essay planning; others use them far more sparingly. How often you use them will depend on how well they suit the way your mind works, so practising a few will give you a sense of whether they will be useful to you.

The best use of brainstorms in an exam is to reduce your anxiety, as they let you put lots of ideas on paper quickly, so that your brain is less clogged with facts which you fear you might forget. They are also useful in those cases where you are sure you know 90% of what is being asked of you, but you have a niggling feeling that you are missing something: a brainstorm will help it to surface.

Creating a spider chart

▶ As with the brainstorm, put your central idea in a circle in the middle of the page.

▶ In circles ranged around the central idea, and joined to it by connecting lines, place the ideas (usually no more than six or so for an exam) that naturally arise from this central point. These are the 'feet' of the 'spider'.

▶ From these 'feet', make more circles and place all of the subsidiary ideas that arise from each of your main points.

▶ Once you have a complete set of ideas set out in this way, you will be able to add more facts to each area of the spider chart, so that it is as detailed as you need it to be before you start to write.

Spider chart example

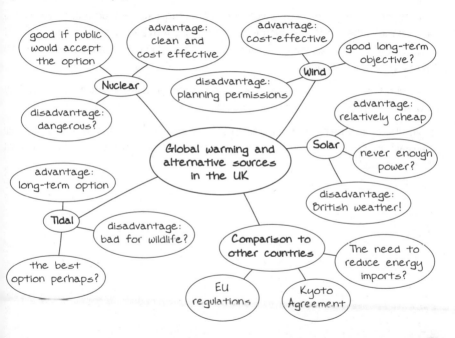

Using a spider chart

For most students the diagram given above is complicated enough, although some students make them far more complicated than this, with arrows showing the order of things and how the ideas connect. Practice will show you how complicated you need to make your spider charts.

Spider charts are useful if you are being asked to create an argument in an essay: they allow you to range freely without ever losing your way.

Spider charts also help you to organise your paragraphs. Each foot of the spider will be a main area of your answer; the small sections off each foot will usually represent a new paragraph.

Creating a flowchart

▸ Your central idea in a flowchart comes in the first box, and is followed by your next idea, in the next box, linked to the first by an arrow.

▸ Put subsidiary ideas or facts in the boxes below each of these main boxes, again joined by an arrow.

▸ You will not expect to record vastly different ideas or facts between a spider chart and a flowchart; the difference lies in the way those ideas are laid out, and the effect this has on your thinking process.

▸ Once your flowchart is complete, you will have a very linear set of ideas, set out in a logical flow of thought. It is this linear progression which is the key to flowcharts: it tends to encourage you to write quite fast and with confidence once the chart is complete.

Flowchart example

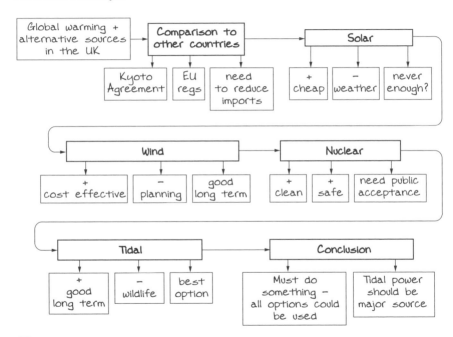

Using a flowchart

Flowcharts are especially useful if you are being asked to describe a process or to show how facts fit together to make a whole picture.

They are effective in short essay answers if you are not being asked to create a complex argument, but instead are simply expected to give a series of facts and ideas.

They also work well if you tend to worry in exams that you might have missed something out. Because each idea flows from the one before it, and is linked to the one after it, it is easy to see at a glance if you have left out a key fact, idea or part of the process.

Creating a mind map

▶ A mind map will be as individual as the person creating it, and there are very few rules to follow. In general, your main idea will still sit centrally on the page, and your subsidiary ideas will come away from that idea.

▶ At each point where you record an idea – so at each section of the mind map – you can usefully use at least three different colours: this helps you to remember more easily what you have written or drawn. In revision this is obviously useful, but it also helps you in an exam, where a quick glance at your mind map will imprint the ideas on your brain.

▶ In the example I have given here there are words and illustrations, usually connected by lines, but you need not include any words if you find it easier to use just pictures, and you could use symbols to connect ideas if you find that easier than using lines. As with all of these methods, practice will help to show you what works best for you.

Mind map example

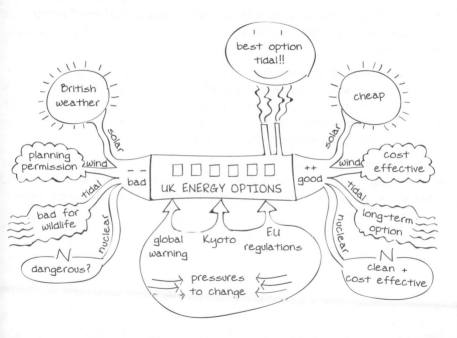

Using a mind map

A mind map can be slower to produce than either a spider chart or a flowchart, but you are less likely to change your mind as you go along, so overall it is not going to slow you down in an exam.

Mind maps are useful, of course, for planning essays and so you will use them in your revision and the exam. However, spider charts and flowcharts are usually quicker to produce, so you might tend to use these as your main methods for quick essay plans as you revise. The greatest benefit of mind maps is that they really do help you to remember complicated series of facts and ideas.

It is for this reason that, as well as your usual revision cards, which list the information you are trying to remember, you might also want to introduce some mind map cards, which would give you an overview of an area, showing how everything is connected.

Changing your mind

Spider charts and flowcharts are intended to help you to test your ideas, and to see how they might fit together, along with the facts, to make a whole. For this reason, it is always going to be good to keep an open mind, to be prepared to change your mind as you go along. In come cases, it is also useful to create one main chart, and then a series of smaller charts to show the detail of some of the more challenging sections of an area.

Your know-it gremlin will help you here: if you look at your plan and are pleased with its shape and detail, your gremlin will be whispering in your ear again, saying 'Well done – you know it!'

In revision, you can change your mind as often as you like, and this is all to the good: it shows that you are developing your ideas and incorporating new facts and theories into your overall view. In an exam you don't have time to keep on changing your mind, but it is still important to be open to the possibility of change and to be prepared to cross out a plan and start again if you really feel that it is not going to work. The few minutes spent on creating a new plan will save you far more time as you write your answer.

The dangers of list plans

Many of us (myself included) enjoy making list plans: simply jotting down a series of headings and sub-headings and adding a few bullet points beneath each to flesh out the ideas.

This method has its benefits: it is quick and usually produces a neat, logical plan – but it also has dangers. It is far more likely to allow you to miss out a whole section of an answer because you are producing it quickly and it is difficult to see at a glance if you have missed something out.

List plans have their place. If you are writing a short answer and feel confident that you have all of the material at your fingertips, they can work well. If you are producing a more complex or lengthy answer, or you have any doubts about how to arrange your material, it is a good insurance policy to use one of the other methods listed here, just to ensure that nothing is left out; if you find it easier to write from a list plan, it will take only a few moments to convert a plan to a list, and then you can work from it with confidence.

Timed essay plans

At first, you will probably want to practise essay planning with no time restrictions, so that you get to know which planning methods suit you best. To find out how well you can use your material in an area, untimed essay plans will always serve you well, but you might also want to practise some timed essay plans, to get you ready for the real thing. I will go through exam timing with you more fully on Day 13, but at this stage we can focus on the planning.

Take *10 minutes* for each essay plan and divide your time:

1 minute to look at the question carefully, to make sure you have grasped all of its implications.

2 minutes to make a six-point list of the key points you want to make.

5 minutes to work this list up into a full plan, using whichever method you prefer.

2 minutes to add any extra detail which comes to you once the plan is complete – dates, quotes, names, extra facts or theories.

Finally, check back to the question: do you think you have answered it fully enough?

What about revision groups?

Revising can leave you feeling isolated, which is not good for morale. Although you should not expect too much from joining a revision group, it can be helpful to share your thoughts on the exams, and so they are worth considering as a source of support.

For some students, revision groups can be a good thing, but think first:

1 How much time do you have to spend meeting with the group?
2 When you leave, do you feel that it was time well spent?
3 Is the group boosting your confidence, or getting you down?
4 Is the group revising together in a way that suits you?

If your answers show up a problem, you might want to abandon the idea altogether, or you could consider setting up an online revision group, which you can dip in and out of when you have a little free time, but which you do not feel obliged to contact if you are not finding it useful at any stage.

Taking stock

You have worked through the repetitious learning stage – well done! Now your revision has become far more active – brainstorming, making essay plans and reducing your revision cards. All of this activity will help to keep you motivated.

Day 7

Things to do today

☐ Rest.

☐ Rest.

☐ Rest.

I know it sounds too good to be true, but it is essential that you take some time out to rest. Your brain needs a break, and time to assimilate the material which you have been revising. Even if you feel you are behind in your revision tasks, try to force yourself into a day off – you really do need it.

For some people this means a day of doing nothing much at all, but for most of us it is better to plan a rest day in advance, so that you make the most of it and reduce your stress levels.

Planning a rest day

If you prefer a more structured rest day, try these out:

1 The night before, plan what you hope to achieve in the day (*not* revision tasks!).

2 Do not get up early – even an extra half an hour in bed will feel like a treat.

3 Work through all of the tasks on your list in the morning – this way you will reduce the pressure when you get back to revision, but give yourself a time limit of just a few hours.

4 Relax completely however you prefer – a nice lunch, a walk, a long bath, watching daytime TV. You will be amazed at how often great thoughts pop into your mind when you are doing nothing.

5 Have a note pad ready to jot down any stray thoughts to do with revision. Note them; then forget them for the rest of the day.

6 Try to spend the afternoon/evening socialising with family or friends, and ask everyone to avoid mentioning revision unless you bring it up – this is the time to forget about it completely.

7 Ideally, get a reasonably early night.

Six more ways to feel good

A rest day will always be beneficial: it is getting back to the revision that can be a problem. You have broken the rhythm of your work and it can seem a real slog after your rest day. Here is how to get over the hurdle:

1 Make a list of the order of your tasks on your first day back.
2 By now, the variety of revision tasks is increasing, so produce a timetable for the day, showing when you are going to do different types of task, and include as much variety as you can.
3 If you do not bounce back easily, do not be too hard on yourself – congratulate yourself for every task you complete.
4 If you do not complete every task, focus at the end of the day on what you have achieved – you will catch up with yourself on the following day as long as you do not lose heart.
5 Reduce the amount of time you usually spend on each task before you move on to another type of revision task.
6 Be prepared to have a longer revision day with far more breaks in it. You will achieve the same amount as normal, but without too much stress.

Things to do today

☐ Reduce your revision notes for Section 5 of your material to revision cards.

☐ Reduce Section 6 of your material to revision notes.

☐ Keep reducing your pile of revision cards (as many as you have time to do).

☐ Keep going with some general essay plans.

☐ Begin working on past papers.

General essay plans will always be useful, but by now you will need also to look at past papers and give yourself some practice with the real thing.

Using past papers

Get hold of as many exam papers as you can: these might be past papers, or examples given to you by your tutor. You might also find past papers from similar courses to yours on internet sites. You have already looked at some past papers on Day 1, to get a sense of where you are going. Now you need to work through them with revision in mind:

▸ There is no need to time yourself; just work through and answer the questions as well as you can and then note where you need to go back and do more work.

▸ There is also no need to produce very detailed answers: just a list of the points you would include, or an essay plan, will be enough to guide you.

▸ Try not to get stressed about the perfect answer; instead, work through a whole paper at a time, then go back and decide where your weaknesses (if any) lie.

▸ Be bold: assess the paper in its entirety and only make a note of areas where you are absolutely sure you need to do more work.

▸ For these areas, pull out the fuller revision cards which you discarded earlier (and, if you really need to, your notes on the subject area) and spend time rereading and testing yourself.

▸ As soon as you feel confident, discard the cards and only pick them up again if that area trips you up later in a practice answer.

The art of procrastination

'Procrastination' is our ability to be very busy doing nothing much, and we often become masters of this during revision time. Many of us, at the end of a day's revision, find our books ordered alphabetically on the shelf, our emails sorted into files, our pets (or even our neighbour's pets) walked for several miles and our distant friends and relatives delighted by our unexpected phone call. We also find that the 'to do' list for the day has not dwindled much at all!

We all need to procrastinate a bit – we are not learning machines, after all, and procrastination can be a positive force in revision. As you procrastinate, your mind ticks over with all of the things you have learnt recently, and you find that you go back to revision knowing more than you thought. This is why those who enjoy computer games or are learning to play the piano are often amazed at how well they come on once they have left it alone for a day.

So, a little procrastination is good, but you must be vigilant …

Anti-procrastination checklist

- Decide in advance when you are going to take breaks – and stick to those times.
- Turn off your mobile when you are trying to focus on a task.
- Never 'nip onto' a social network site like Facebook – you can lose an hour before you even notice.
- Try using the same procrastination task every time you need a break – this might be working your way through a huge pile of washing, or answering three emails in each break (but no more) or texting friends (and then you turn your mobile off again). The rhythm will help to keep you on track.
- If you find yourself looking out of the window far too much, or rereading the same revision card several times, take a proper break and allow yourself a set amount of time before you try again.
- Vary your tasks – always. This helps to keep you interested in what you are doing.
- Save some 'easy tasks' for each day, so that you can lower the pressure whilst still getting through the work.
- Have a snack or sweet drink beside you to keep you going – we all work poorly on low blood sugar.
- If you are losing your way, a brainstorm of the area you are working on can help bring you back on track.

Things to do today

☐ Reduce your revision notes for Section 6 of your material to revision cards.

☐ Reduce Section 7 of your material to revision notes.

☐ Keep reducing your pile of revision cards (as many as you have time to do).

☐ Go back to past essays for inspiration.

So far, you have been focusing on gathering and remembering information and putting it to use. Today, take some time to read a few of the essays you have produced during your course. It is a good way to remind yourself of how you have used information in the past, and could inspire you as you remember all the good work that you have done already.

When you find an essay that covers material likely to come up in the exam, try making a spider chart or mind map of the essay on a revision card, so that you can remember exactly how you did it.

How to tackle a seen exam

There are two ways in which your tutors might try to help you: by giving you an exam paper in advance, so that you can prepare your answer thoroughly before the exam (a 'seen exam'), and by letting you take key texts into the exam (an 'open book exam'). Both of these situations bring dangers with them.

For a seen exam, writing out the whole essay beforehand and trying to memorise it can cause problems – if you lose your place in the exam and cannot remember it exactly, you run the risk of missing out whole sections and panicking. Instead, write a good opening and closing and leave the rest in plan form, so that you know the material, but are not tied to the words. You will need your know-it gremlin close at hand for this part, reassuring you that a plan is sufficient, that you will know what to write in the exam because you know the material behind the plan.

You are already making essay plans as part of your revision, so this need be no different, except that you will be adding more detail than usual and you will have your books and notes to guide you as you make the plan.

For the seen exam question 'Discuss the advances in state education during the late nineteenth century' you would produce something like this for your opening paragraph:

> *Various forms of education were already in place by the late nineteenth century. Dame schools, workers' education programmes and fee-paying grammar schools all existed. The Victorian Age was one of advancement, and education took its place in that march of progress.*

This opening shows that you have a good overall grasp of the subject area; it also gives an indication of the historical approach you intend to take. It acts as a spring-board to the body of your answer …

The spider chart on the next page shows how you might structure the remainder of the essay.

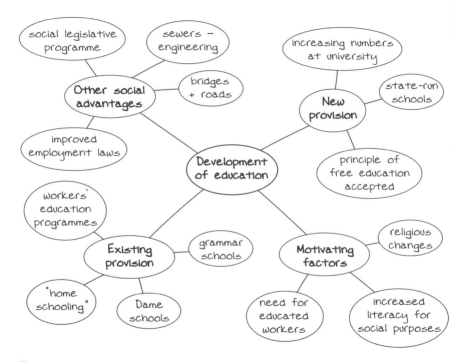

- social legislative programme
- sewers – engineering
- bridges + roads
- increasing numbers at university
- state-run schools
- Other social advantages
- New provision
- improved employment laws
- Development of education
- principle of free education accepted
- workers' education programmes
- grammar schools
- Existing provision
- Motivating factors
- religious changes
- "home schooling"
- Dame schools
- need for educated workers
- increased literacy for social purposes

Your closing section must also be strong and may include a paragraph reiterating the main points you have made. The final sentence must be firm and show your overview of the topic. The closing to this essay could be something like this:

> *Today we still reap the benefits of Victorian progress. Many of the sewers under our big cities are Victorian and so are some of our major bridges. However, unlike these successful and long-lasting structures upon which we rely every day, state education still has some way to go before it can fulfil the dreams of our forbears.*

This closing is not introducing new evidence: it merely sums up your overall points and should leave the examiner feeling that you have had enough time in the exam to say all that you wanted to say.

How to tackle an open book exam

For an open book exam, you need to be selective in your preparation and disciplined in the exam. You will be told which books you can take in with you, and it is unlikely that you will be able to make notes in them, although it is usually acceptable to place markers in the books and/or underline key passages. Be sparing: only mark up those sections you really need, and you will identify these from your essay planning as you revise.

In the exam, spending ages looking for the perfect quote might take too much time away from actually writing your exam answer. When you write essay plans as part of your revision, practise looking up the odd fact or quote, and get into the habit of using the book as sparingly as possible: it is only there for the odd reference or to guide you if you really get stuck.

Reducing anxiety

Being nervous about an exam is always a good thing: it means that you are ready to go, keen to succeed and have enough adrenaline in your system to keep your mind sharp. Being too nervous, however, can hinder your performance. Your aim is to be nervous but prepared. Your revision tasks will prepare you; the event will make you nervous; the tips below will help to control your nerves.

1 Always know all the practical details of the exam before the day, so that you do not waste your nerves on panicking about where you are going, when, and what will happen to you when you get there.

2 Have one or two 'last minute' revision cards with you as you wait to go into the exam. These are the cards which contain information that you simply cannot seem to remember, and will be left outside the room as you go in.

3 Nerves make your mouth dry and can lead to dehydration: take a water bottle into each exam with you.

4 If your blood sugar is likely to dip too low, have something easy to eat (a banana, raisins, a snack bar) ready for the minutes before the exam.

5 If you are not sleeping well, try a nap after each exam: much better than endless discussions with friends about how well you did.

Relaxation techniques

As you wait to go into an exam, there are some techniques you can use to keep your nerves under control:

1 Sit down with your back straight and your feet slightly apart.
2 Spread your fingers wide and rest them lightly on your thighs.
3 Wiggle your toes: they will probably be bunched up with nerves.
4 Relax your tongue: it is probably sticking to the roof of your mouth.
5 Use your right-hand fingers to firmly press along the top of the left-hand side of your back, at the top of your shoulder blades.
6 Keep this kneading motion going across your shoulder and down the back of your left arm, right down to your wrist.

diaphragm

7 Repeat this process using your left hand on your right side.
8 Breathe out naturally and just close your mouth. Refuse to breathe until you really feel you have to take a breath, then simply open your mouth without any effort to breathe in. Your diaphragm will do all of the work for you, and you will take a naturally calming, deep breath.

Taking stock

You are about to move into the final phase of your revision, and you can be proud of what you have achieved so far. All of your hard work is now going to pay off, as it all fits into place.

Things to do today

☐ Reduce your revision notes for Section 7 of your material to revision cards.

☐ Reduce Section 8 of your material to revision notes.

☐ Keep reducing your pile of revision cards (as many as you have time to do).

☐ Give yourself a mock exam.

A mock exam moves you onto the next stage of your revision. Planning essays is useful for remembering; a mock exam will:

▶ prepare you for how you might feel in the exam

▶ help you to see how well you remember under pressure

▶ give you a sense of how much you can produce against the clock

▶ help to familiarise you with the process of the exam.

How to give yourself a mock essay exam

1 Allow yourself the correct amount of time to do the mock exam, with no interruptions.
2 Put away every scrap of revision material you have.
3 Answer the exam question to time: it does not matter if you have tackled the question before in your revision; this will feel different and now it is against the clock.
4 Use the time to plan, write and check the answer, just as you would in an exam. So, for an hour's essay exam you would aim to plan for the first 10 minutes, write for 45 minutes and check for the last 5 minutes. You can alter this timing accordingly for a short answer exam.
5 If you get stuck, resolutely push yourself to keep going, just like in an exam.
6 When you have finished, take a break and then go back and check:
   ▶ Did you make a strong opening and ending?
   ▶ Did your plan work? Did you miss out anything vital?
   ▶ Did you have enough time to finish the answer?

Beyond these three points there is no need to worry too much: even if the answer is not as perfect as you would like, you have mastered the basics of the exam, and the rest will come as you continue to revise.

How to give yourself a mock multiple choice exam

1 As with the essay exam, you will put away all of your revision material and just face the question.
2 Some of the questions will be fairly easy for you, and answering these first will give you confidence. Do not be tempted to rush too fast, though: it is easy to lose points by making careless mistakes.
3 For the more challenging questions, you will usually be offered one answer option that is obviously wrong, one that is wrong as soon as you study it in more detail, one that is very nearly right and one that is the correct answer. Focus on these last two.
4 If you are struggling, writing the options out on your scrap paper in the exam can help to clarify things for you.
5 Once you think you have completed the paper, go back and check that you have answered every single question, and clearly marked the right box.
6 Finally, check each answer, for both the easier and harder questions, just to make sure that you have not missed anything.
7 Once you have done this: stop. The most dangerous time in a multiple choice exam is the last minute – you may decide to change some of your answers, but find that you alter your choice to the wrong answer because you have had time to doubt yourself.

What mock exams do for you

Sometimes you can complete a mock exam and feel elated: it has all gone perfectly and you are delighted with your answer. Sometimes it can leave you despairing. Neither of these is a true response since each is created from the pressure you have just put on yourself. That is what mock exams are designed to do: get you used to the pressure so that you are less panicky when you go into the exam room.

When you come to look back at your mock exam answers, you will find that they are never absolutely right or absolutely wrong; just as in an exam, your performance will differ each time. That is why it is essential to check your mock exam answers as you move forward: to guide you in your revision, but also to remind you how far you have come. Again, keep your know-it gremlin beside you, so that you can be confident about what most of your mock exams will show you: that you have mastered a good part of the material you need.

From now on you will aim to do mock exams alongside your other revision tasks, so that you keep focused on the ultimate goal: the exam itself.

Things to do today

☐ Reduce your revision notes for Section 8 of your material to revision cards.

☐ Tidy up your work space.

☐ STOP for the day.

This is, deliberately, an easier day than most. You have been working hard, with an increasing number of tasks each day, and you need to take stock. Tidying away your discarded revision cards, filing all of the revision notes you no longer need and throwing away all the rubbish that has accumulated will keep things in control and so clear your head for the final push before the exams. It will also give you time to think about your exam strategy.

Exam strategy

Mock exams of just one question will take you only so far: mock exams of entire papers will help you develop your strategy. There is no 'right way' to master exam papers, so you have decisions to make:

1 In a blended exam, which section would you prefer to tackle first (multiple choice, short answer, longer essay)?

2 In an essay exam paper, would you feel most comfortable giving your strongest answer first, or starting with your weakest and moving on from there?

3 Do you prefer to plan all of your answers first, then write out the complete answers? Or would you rather take each answer in itself, plan it and write it before you move on?

Try these different approaches in your mock exams, or think back to previous exams, remembering what worked for you, and plan your strategy in advance, so that you have the best chance of success in each exam.

Knowing when and why to stop

Today has been an easier day, giving your brain the chance to relax a little. Like the rest day on Day 7, your mind will have been assimilating material and sorting it even without you realising it. Going into an exam as a frazzled, exhausted wreck is not going to do you any good: it is better to know a little less and be fresh and ready to use it to maximum effect than to know much more and be too tired to use it.

From now on, you must trust yourself. There will still be revision tasks to do, and you have plenty of time left to master more material, but if you get tired or find that you are busy getting nowhere, ask yourself these questions:

1 *Is it difficult to focus because, actually, I already know this material?* Be firm with yourself and put it to one side.
2 *Have I just got bored with this task?* Move on to another task and come back to this later.
3 *Have I lost motivation with the whole process?* Take a decent break (several hours if you need it) and then try again.
4 *Are my nerves stopping me from thinking straight?* This is the perfect time to prac- tise the relaxation techniques from Day 9.

Day 12

Things to do today

☐ Make a final check on your revision cards, focusing especially on those you made yesterday.

☐ Keep reducing your pile of revision cards. It will not matter if you cannot do this for all of your cards – just as many as you have time to do.

☐ Make a 'last minute' card (or several) for each section of your material.

☐ Take stock of your position.

How to know how much you know: sorting the cards

Until now, you have been sorting material, reducing it, and using it to make essay plans and do mock exams. In these last couple of days you might want to carry on with your essay plans, but your key focus is best placed on assessing what you know. There is a system for this:

1 Put the pile of revision cards for each section of material on the table in front of you. (Put your 'last minute' cards for each section to one side – you will only need these just before each exam.)

2 Some piles will be larger than others, depending on how much you knew already and how much time you have been able to spend reducing each set of cards, and that is no problem.

3 Take the first pile, glance at the title of each card and try reciting what you think is on that card. You are unlikely ever to be perfect at this, and there is no need to be.

4 If you feel you know nearly all of the material on the card, put it on one pile; if you feel much less confident about the contents of the card, put it on another pile.

5 There will probably be a third pile here too – the cards that you might or might not know well, but that you now think are not really essential because they contain material that you do not realistically expect to use in the exam. These are not wasted cards: by making them you have ensured that you know some of the material, enough to refer to it in passing if you need to.

How to know how much you know: mastering the cards

For each section of material, you will now have three piles of cards:

1 The pile of cards with material you have chosen not to use in the exam, except in passing or in an emergency, can be firmly placed to one side.

2 For each section, you can ignore for now the pile of cards where you are confident of the material: you can look at these every now and then tomorrow, and between exams, as a confidence boost and reminder. Keep your know-it gremlin close by you for this: you do know this material.

3 With the pile of cards where you are less familiar with the material, check each one and be ruthless: can you realistically expect to remember this card for the exam, or should it be added to your discarded pile?

You are now left with a pile of cards which you need to tackle head on ...

What to do with the last pile

1 Use those cards with material you absolutely have to learn, because you are sure it will come up in the exam or it is part of an area you want to cover, as 'flash cards'.

2 For each 'flash card', glance at the title, cover the card, recite the material as best you can, check how well you have done. There is no easy way to do this, and it can be a little tedious, but repeating this process over and over will give you the best chance of remembering the material.

3 Once you feel confident about the material, you can add that card to your pile of those cards with which you feel confident.

It is unlikely that you will go into any exam having learnt all of the material on every card, but that will not be a problem: you will have mastered enough material to use it well and produce a good exam answer.

Openings and endings

Beginning an exam answer well and polishing it off with a flourish will always impress examiners. It shows that you have strong ideas, a clear sense of how to express them and that you are in control of your subject. Openings and endings are also a great way to revise in this, the final stage of your revision. To practise, you can use past or example papers or, at this stage, you will be able to make up your own questions, similar to those you have worked on before.

1 Give yourself a time limit (probably no more than 15–20 minutes).
2 There is no need to do a full plan, but brainstorm your answer if you feel it will help.
3 Write out the opening paragraph – use bullet points to make your ideas clearer if this makes it easier.
4 Write out your ending to the answer – this might be no more than a sentence or two, summing up what you would have covered.

In those 15 minutes or so, you have reminded yourself of the area, decided how to tackle it and effectively revised it all in one swift exercise.

Some people find strong openings and endings easy, others struggle a bit. By doing a few of these in the day before each exam you will feel far more confident as you face each question.

Taking stock

You have done nearly all you can now to ensure your success. Although you will keep working your material to keep your confidence levels up, from now on it is much more about achieving focus, being firm in your aims and clear about what you are doing. So, it is important to take a moment to take stock of what you have achieved so far:

Things to do today

☐ Make a final check on the exam arrangements: time, place and how you are getting there. This sounds so simple, but it is far too easy to get it wrong.

☐ Keep on looking at your revision cards, to brush up on some final material.

☐ Practise openings and endings for exam answers.

☐ Buy some high-energy snacks for tomorrow.

☐ Take a night off, if you can.

And the first thing to do in the exam is …

It is a good idea to have clearly in your mind exactly how you will face the beginning of an exam:

▶ Remember how you planned to divide your time between planning, writing and checking. Ideally, 10 minutes planning, 45 minutes writing, 5 minutes checking for each hour of an essay exam.

▶ Read ALL the questions twice, putting a star beside the ones you think you want to answer. Do not be afraid to ask the invigilators if you think there is something wrong with the paper.

▶ If the paper is multiple choice, use the strategy outlined on Day 10.

▶ Unburden your mind of all the 'rubbish' that will get in the way – do this by jotting down the material from your 'last minute' card.

▶ Read the questions again, confirming your choice.

▶ Remember how any mock exams that you gave yourself felt at this point: this will help to calm your nerves and focus your mind.

▶ Decide in advance whether to plan each answer at the beginning, or whether to plan each essay as you work through the paper.

- Decide in advance whether it is better for you to answer your 'strongest' question first or last.

- Make a six-point plan straight away of your key points: this might be a brainstorm or just a list (3 minutes).

- Read the question again.

- 'Flesh out' your six-point plan (7 minutes). Use your preferred planning method for this stage. Does it still make sense? At this stage, include a note of quotes, dates, other texts that you might mention, your conclusion etc.

- Go back to your 'rubbish dump' and see if anything from there needs to be included.

Only now do you begin to write, or perhaps to plan your other answers. This takes courage; many of the people around you will already be scribbling away madly. Hold your nerve and only write when you are sure you are ready to go … your answer will be better for it.

The night before the exam

What to do …

It is easy to say 'take the night off' – it is far harder to do in reality. Remember that by now you will have all the material you are likely to be able to retain already in your head: endlessly going over and over it will make little difference.

If you know you're likely to work yourself into a frenzy of nerves to no good purpose the night before an exam, it might be a good idea to plan a low-key evening out with friends, perhaps to see a film that you know will distract you nicely.

If you know that being completely away from your work will be more stressful than not, then give yourself the easiest possible revision time by just having some of your most important revision cards beside you as you try to relax. That way, you can always reassure yourself of how far you have come, and this will help to keep you calm.

What not to do …

Try not to leave your evening entirely unplanned. If you have no idea how you are going to occupy your time, you are more likely to drift about in a state of anxiety.

Look after yourself physically. An excess of food or alcohol or a late night is likely to impair your performance.

Encourage friends and family to text you their good luck messages rather than calling you. An hour's conversation with someone reminiscing about 'my exam disasters of yesteryear' is unlikely to help.

All the questions might be in Greek! Or Chinese! Or Riddles!

Avoid any discussion at all about the exam with anyone else who is taking it. If you realise you need to know a specific detail about the practicalities, that is fine, but talking at length about the exam is more likely to scare than to comfort you. At this stage, rumours about the exam and what is required of you will be flying about, and will only distract you.

Day 14: exam day!

Things to do today

☐ Eat something – anything – to prepare you for the day ahead. If you cannot manage a full meal, snack on foods that will keep your energy levels high.

☐ Aim to get to the exam room no more than 30 minutes before the exam. This will give you time to check that it is the right place, so that you can wander off for a while, but much longer than this spent waiting around will just increase your nerves.

☐ If you need reassurance, check over your 'last minute' card for the exam, and remind yourself of the plan of attack outlined below.

In the exam …

Before you start to write, follow the strategy outlined in Day 13.

When you are writing:

▶ Work from your more detailed plan, but keep an eye on the time. Be prepared to abandon a point in the best way you can if you are running too far over on time, but allow it to flow naturally for as long as you can.

- If you have to abandon a point, leave enough space so that you can direct the marker to work that you add later on.
- If you get really short on time, you might need to direct the marker back to your plan so that s/he can see where you would have gone.

If you wobble:

- Several peculiar things can happen to your brain in an exam:
  - You seem to be writing complete rubbish.
  - You lose the point of what you wanted to say.
  - You start to doubt that you have answered the right question.

In fact, these are unlikely to be real problems, in that none of them will be a true reflection of the situation. What is really happening is that you are getting tired, or nerves are getting the better of you, or you have just had to go through too many exams in a short space of time. If this happens to you, STOP WRITING for a few seconds, take a breath and check back to your plan. This will ground you back in your main six points and the whole process will become easier again.

- If, in the few seconds that you have taken a break, you decide that you really have gone off course, close the point you are making as soon as you can and move firmly on to your next point. This will probably appear seamless in your final script, but it will ensure that you keep on track.

And towards the end ...

▶ Checking is always going to be important, but you have relatively little time to do this in an exam. If you have 5 minutes, you will have time to read your whole script through for errors and inconsistency. This is going to be a better bet than simply continuing to write until the very end of the exam.

▶ If you are running out of time, and have only a few minutes to do some final checking, abandon the idea of reading through the entire script and instead look for typical weak points in each answer:

The opening: does it say what you mean?

The conclusion: is it strong enough?

Titles and dates: are they accurate?

Names and technical terms: are they right?

Blanks and spaces: can you fill them in now?

Gaps left for more writing: do you have time now?

Two-thirds of the way through: did you have a moment of madness?

And when it is over …

Forget it! You know that you have worked hard for this exam. If you have a specific concern (did I get a particular fact right?) then you might check with a couple of friends, but beyond this, post-mortems are rarely a good idea.

The following day, however, you might like to reflect upon your strengths and weaknesses whilst they are fresh in your mind. Make a note of what you intend to do differently in future exams. It is surprising how quickly the details of the experience fade from your mind, but notes made now will help you to focus your energy in future exams.

If you have several days between each exam, follow the steps on Days 12 and 13 to keep your mind ticking over, but make sure you build some decent rest breaks into your schedule.

You are here because you deserve to be. Contrary to popular belief, exams are an exciting time – you are finally getting the chance to show how well you have mastered your subject. You will do your best and produce the results that you need …

Good Luck!

Index